JACK VETTRIANO

A MAN'S WORLD

For Amanda Jane

Jack Vettriano

JACK VETTRIANO

A MAN'S WORLD

PAVILION

Previous page: Seaside Sharks

man

- noun (pl. men)

1 an adult human male.
2 a husband or lover.
3 a figure or token used in a board game.

My work relies heavily on narrative though I never much like to discuss the narrative, preferring as I do to allow the viewer to compose their own, perhaps more personal scenarios.

Men are less complete than women. Our wiring systems are geared for life on earth two million years ago. To have half the population of the world emotionally underdeveloped is an inescapable part of the human condition. So man soldiers on.

A Man's World contains some of the images which to my way of thinking best represent the emotional turmoil of man; from predatory to vulnerable, from cruel to sensitive and from hungry to bloated – my men are thus defined.

'I wish the women would hurry up and take over…it's going to happen so lets get it over with. Then we can finally recognize that women really are the minds and force that holds everything together and men are really gossips and artists.' Leonard Cohen. (*Leonard Cohen in his own words*, Jim Devlin, Omnibus Press)

Bluebird at Bonneville

Pendine Beach

The Clouds are Gathering

Lazy Hazy Days

Suddenly One Summer II

Jealous Heart

The Billy Boys

Amateur Philosophers

The Drifter

Gambling Boys

The Star Café

Bad, Bad Boys

On the Make

Evening Racing

Man Pursued

All Systems Go

The City Café

Sometimes it's a Man's World

The Trap

A Test of True Love

The Cigar Divan

Fetish

Cleo and The Boys

An Assignation

Betrayal, The First Kiss

The Purple Cat

The Ballroom Spy

Incident at the Blue Lagoon

The Set Up

Night Geometry

Heaven on Earth

Private Dancer

The Altar of Memory

Another Kind of Love

A Kind of Loving

The Sparrow and The Hawk

The Cocktail Shaker

Heatwave

On Parade

Soho Nights

An Imperfect Past

Dancer for Money

Legs Eleven

Devotion

Beautiful Losers

The Master of Ceremonies

Setting New Standards

Wicked Games

The Parlour of Temptation

Heaven or Hell

Along Came a Spider

At Last, My Lovely

Passion Overflow

The Party's Over

Game On

A Mutual Understanding

Sailor's Toy

The Same Old Game

Between Darkness and Dawn

Master of Ceremonies (Study)

Pincer Movement

The Embrace of the Spider

A Sinister Turn of Emotion

His Favourite Girl

Round Midnight

Just The Way It Is

Under Cover of the Night

A Very Married Woman

A Terrible Beauty

Heartbreak Hotel

Rough Trade

The Water Babies

Bad Boy Blues

Motel Love

The Remains of Love

The Temptress

Studio Afternoon

The Artist and Model

The Critical Hour of 3am

Index of paintings

First published in Great Britain in 2009
by Pavilion

An imprint of the Anova Books Company Ltd
10 Southcombe Street, London W14 0RA

Paintings © Jack Vettriano
Design and layout © Pavilion
Designed by Martin Hendry
Jacket Design by Georgina Hewitt

The moral right of the painter has been asserted

A CIP catalogue record for this book is available from the British Library.

ISBN 978 1 86205 856 9

Printed and bound by 1010 Printing International Ltd, China

10 9 8 7 6 5 4 3 2 1

This book can be ordered direct from the publisher. Please contact the Marketing Department.
But try your bookshop first.

www.anovabooks.com

For further information on Jack Vettriano please visit www.jackvettriano.com